ENTERING THE DARKNESS – A P

By

E. P . Kelly

I have always been interested in anything spooky.   As a small child I had various encounters with the spirit world, and as I grew older I visited a spiritualist church. Deciding that it really wasn't for me I completely ignored any signs that the spirit world were giving me. I still believed in the spirit world and knew deep down that when we leave this earth we went on to somewhere else but didn't delve deeper into finding out any more than that.

This all changed when I started seeing spirit in my 30s, firstly out of the corner of my eye when I started working nightshift at a supermarket, my colleague Bev also used to have experiences as we worked on the same department.

I used to see a man in a Blue boiler suit and a cap, at first I thought it was just a residual haunting (like a film being played back) but one night I heard him say my name so he was clearly aware of his surroundings and of me!

Another spirit I sensed to be a lady, I would hear the coat hanger's move and the jewellery used to swing on its own. Most people would be freaked out but to us it was the norm.

I strongly believe that places aren't necessarily haunted, people from the spirit world come back to visit from time to time. Probably keeping an eye on things, or loved ones.

One night at work I saw my auntie that had just passed to spirit earlier that week!

Things progressed from then on, I started visiting Spiritualist churches, I even joined the churches development classes, but I needed hard evidence that the spirit world exists.

I saw a ghost hunt advertised at a local venue and decided to go along. I quite enjoyed it but didn't really like how the 'hunt' was conducted and thought that I could do a better job myself. So, that exactly what I did, searching the internet for local reputedly haunted buildings, I contacted one and booked it. I talked a few friends into chipping in with the cost and we set off armed with a camcorder and a voice recorder.

We had fun that night, not really knowing what we were

doing but a few strange things happened that night. The camcorder turned itself off, not really evidence but it helped set the scene. The next day I decided to start to listen to the voice recorder, and low and behold we had caught the voice of a very miserable sounding man. He had moaned near the voice recorder whilst we weren't anywhere near. Finally, I was on my way to collecting solid evidence that the spirit world existed.

From that moment, my quest for gathering more evidence started, but I had to think of a group name as everywhere I tried to book asked what group name to book it under.

Spectre Detectors was born.....November 2011.

When I look back now and remember how excited I used to get for literally 2 minutes of evidence caught from at least 8 hours of footage, I realise that patience really has been key to getting where we are now. We really have earned our stripes!

A few people have come and gone along the way for various reasons, but Bev has always been by my side helping out where needed.

Right now the group has just the right kind of mix, and this is evident in the amazing evidence that we are capturing on our recording devices. Most of the group are psychic mediums, which is absolutely great and others are sensitive to spirit as we've all learned our own techniques along the way. You will get to know the group as you get an insight into each investigation. We are all extremely comfortable working with spirit, which seems very strange to most people, but to us it's just like talking to someone in another room.

Nearly everyone who joins us one our investigations has a personal experience of some kind, whether it be a touch, smell or feeling. And the gadgets that we use also give spirit a voice and people the chance to experience spirit. There's nothing better than hearing the voice of someone in the spirit world.

We have been featured on a paranormal radio show, been in an American magazine and featured in various newspapers. This is purely because of the evidence that we have been given by spirit.

Here are some of our investigations from the North East of England, not necessarily haunted, as I'm a big believer that spirit will communicate with you no matter where you are. But each venue has a very special place within our hearts, all with an amazing history and each one with very special links to the spirit world.

Francis, Brother Thomas, and Brother Samuel. We picked up the presence of a dog and lots of the group experienced feeling it around their legs.

People also experienced feeling sick, which is what the spirit box had said earlier.

We decided to end the evening with a final séance in the bar, and the spirit box said various words including "what are you doing, yes, bless him, bitches and shut up", it also gave how many spirit people in the room and that age of one of the spirits.

Janette picked up lots of children in the room and that beermats get thrown around (which Chris confirmed).

It was a fantastic investigation, which we conducted over 5 hours and we had been shown some amazing evidence.

The monk in the cellar

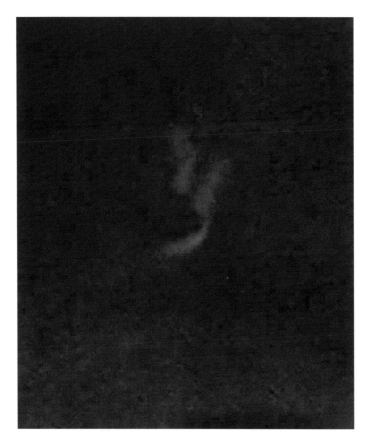

Another monk in the cellar

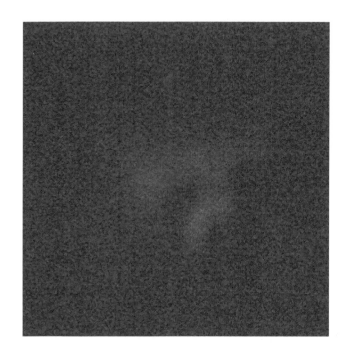

Could this be a dog?

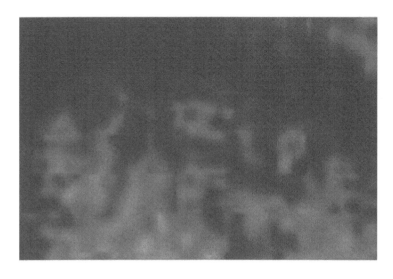

A man (left hand side) and Letters caught on camera

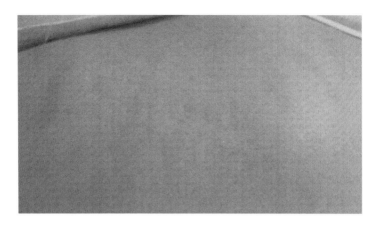

Hannahs back – showing the lashing marks

The tunnel entrance inside the cellar

THE DUN COW PUB AT DURHAM

I contacted Jill the landlady of the Dun Cow at Durham and asked if we could investigate The Dun Cow pub. This fantastic pub is was built in the late 17th century/early 18th century and is known as the hangman's pub as it was built opposite Durham Prison and the hangman used to go there for a tipple before doing his job. The crowd used to stand outside too to watch the execution. The term "money for old rope" comes from the hangman's noose, the hangman used to cut the rope into pieces and sell it as memorabilia from a hanging.

The pub is part of various ghost Walks so has a reputation for being haunted so we were very excited to carry out an investigation.

Jill (the landlady) was happy to give us access to every part of the pub and living quarters as she and the staff have had their own ghostly experiences so were keen to find out more about who else resides there. Jill had invited some of her friends who were interested to stay behind during the investigation.

We were joined by Dean Jameson who is a fantastic medium based in the North East.

Dean immediately picked up that it was was a red light in the upstairs windows, so knew that this was a brothel at some point. As soon as you walk into the inn, you are immediately taken back in time. Its features are still the same as hundreds of years ago. And you immediately sense that you aren't alone, but you also sense that it's a nice atmosphere and that there's nothing negative within the building. But you do get a sense of sadness!

Once we had been shown around, we started to set up the equipment including the night vision cctv, along with other recording devices in the most active areas and started our investigation upstairs in the passageway.

We began calling out and immediately picked up on the working girls. Janette sensed that the children of these girls used to get locked in a small room attached to the main bedroom whilst they had clients. She also knew that Jill had probably heard movement in that room (which Jill later confirmed).

We picked up the names Elizabeth, Betty and Rose. We also picked up that there had been a back street abortion carried out there too.   Also the word soldiers came through the sprit box, and I later discovered that the pub was used as a billet in WW1 from 1914-16.

Janette also caught a heat source coming through the wall with the thermal imaging camera, and it looked like a person.

We were also getting tap responses when we were asking questions.

Some of the group decided to go and investigate the attic.   This fantastic area still had the original window and wooden beams, half of the attic was out of bounds as it didn't look very safe and looked as if at some point there had been a fire.

There were hundreds of old nails in the wooden beam, which looked very interesting but fairly creepy!

The group started calling out in the hope of communicating with the spirits, and straight away picked up on a lady that had been held captive in the attic.   They felt like this lady was from a foreign country and was held against her will.   She was a sex slave, and had a broken heart.   They also felt that the nails in the wooden beams were some way of counting the days that she was held there, and that she was possibly drugged.   Lots of light anomalies were picked up on cctv and various taps and bangs in response to questions.

We decided to investigate downstairs in the lounge area, we picked up a lady with very scruffy clothes that dated from the 1700s, a man that sexually assaulted a lady and could possibly have killed her.   The group also picked up that there had been squatters there and that they had maybe done a oujia board there at some point. 1875 was on important year, possible for an important hanging. They picked up on a very thin little boy, who wasn't properly looked after.   Janette sensed that things moved in the bar, including beer mats, which again Jill confirmed.   She picked up that it's a former landlady and that she makes herself known. There have been sightings of a figure of a lady standing behind the bar.

From the lounge, we moved into the cellar, where we picked up that there is a lot of activity, people being touched etc.   And the group sensed that there had been a fight and the name Tomlinson. It was hard to hear, with the workings of the cellar but we did experience being touched. Our clothes were being tugged.

From the cellar we moved into the bar area where Dean sensed a man with a walking stick.   A miser with a heart complaint that had passed to spirit within the last 10 years, and he was a nervous person. Jill confirmed that there has infact been sightings of a man sat in the chair.   He also picked up that people linked to the court used to drink in the pub and it had a big connection with the building to the left, and that somewhere there is a tunnel that goes to that building.

There's also a little girl that haunts the bar area, and she loves dogs, especially Collies and Labradors.   Rebecca and Joe link with the building and car keys and change go missing. We decided to do a spirit box session and we connected with a hangman.

A few of us (including Jill and a couple of her friends) decided to go into the attic where we did some calling out.   A box full of glasses moved themselves and landed straight onto my foot! One of Jill's friends felt very off balance and decided to leave. Once we had decided it was time to leave the attic and some of the group were climbing down the very steep stairs there was a very loud clatter!

We decided that we had investigated as much as we could and decided to pack up our equipment and do the closing prayer.

When I had watched the footage, we had caught some amazing evidence, including what looked like a heat source peering around the door in the lounge when there wasn't anyone there.   We caught the spirit box sessions on infrared handycam and caught some great orbs on cctv. Again, it was a fantastic investigation for Spectre Detectors. We get to investigate some amazing buildings and are usually the first ever group to do so.

We have been invited back.....will the spirits of the dun cow have more to say???

We certainly hope so!

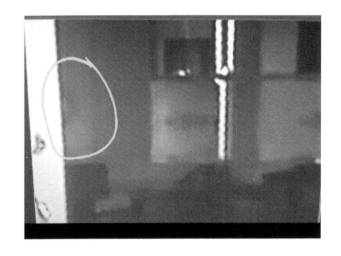

The heat source caught in the bar

Light anomalie caught in the attic

THE HIPPODROME BINGO HALL BISHOP AUCKLAND

After doing previous special events with renowned psychic medium Debra Chalmers, I contacted her about doing another investigation.   Debra told me that she had been visited off my gran and she wanted us to do the 'picture house' at Bishop Auckland.   I knew that the Odeon cinema had been demolished many years before and the only old cinema left in the town was The Hippodrome.

I had contacted the bingo hall a few years before and hadn't had any luck but thought it was worth another try. Luckily the management at Majestic bingo gave us not only their consent but their full support.

A few of the staff members had seen the Grey lady and were quite frightened, but they wanted to find out who she is.

The hall was originally opened as a cine-variety theatre in 1909 by J.J. Taylor under the supervision of George F Ward for Signor Rino Pepi. It was used as a cinema from the outset and converted into a bingo hall in 1960. The architectural practice of Owen and Ward was a successful Birmingham practice that built many theatres, although this example and the Grade II listed Darlington Civic Theatre are their only surviving auditoria.   Signor Pepi was a theatre impressario who created a chain of music halls across northern England and who developed the 'pepiscope' for showing films, as part of his variety routine.

When it opened, the Hippodrome Theatre was the biggest auditorium in the town seating 1800, and top of the bill on its opening night was the well-known and popular comedian Lil Hawthorne.

Originally, both live entertainment and films were shown indicating that the building was of the cine-variety form of theatre, but by 1914, the building was already mainly used as a cinema and was renamed The Hippodrome Picture House, so this must have been the picture house my gran wanted us to visit!

So, in November 2016, we went to set up the cameras quietly whilst people were playing bingo. The night got off to a great start, as Bev and I were getting our equipment out of the office the door slammed shut behind us.   When we asked staff if they could let us back in, we were told that that doesn't normally happen.

Once the last game was over Debra and the group (which was mainly made up of mediums) started to arrive ready for the long night ahead. We set up cctv in the gods (not open to the public), the 2nd floor, inside one of the royal boxes and on the ground floor.

We started in the lower floor and Debra started to communicate with spirit.   A little boy called James was picked up.   The names Tom and Phillip were also picked up.

Debra was shown a Red cross on the door and felt that it had been used as a hospital at some point, probably during the war.

She picked up a bingo player call Mary and picked up on children that moved or touched people's keys, and felt that they messed around with the computer system. This was confirmed that one of the bingo boards goes off as if someone has won when there's no one there.

Most of the group started to smell TCP, which linked in with the hospital conditions that Debra had picked up on.

The name Eleanor was picked up and Janette picked up the name Thomas White.

It was felt that Eleanor was a singer/actress.   Debra picked up that a man was watching us and she picked up on twins.

Another medium picked up shire horses, and a lad called Edward who worked in the stables.

Debra picked up pipe smoke and chewing tobacco and also a caretaker called Sid.

Debra also picked up on freesia flowers and a lady in a dressing gown.   She's very beautiful and petite, around the time of Bet Davies - 1940's.   She felt that she was a dancer.

Hannah picked up on Florrie who was a singer.

Shayna picked up on Stan, could this be Stan Laurel who

lived in Bishop Auckland?

Debra is also aware of the change of lights in the room.

Debra was aware of a lady called Nell who played bingo but always had a cushion behind her back, one of the group knew the lady and said that she used the cushion so that she could reach the table. She also felt that there had been a fire at the building, or possibly a car fire outside but none of the staff knew if this was correct. She also got the feeling that someone had really bad teeth as hers had started to hurt.

Another medium picked up on an alcoholic, and the name Richard was given.

We decided to try a spirit box session and asked these questions:-

What is your name?....Hannah

How many people are here?.....5

Is Thomas Wright here?.....Yes

Did you work here?.....Yes

Are there children here?....Yes (a childs voice)

Are you going to tell us your name?...Kevin

We could also hear a child crying

Is the Grey lady here?.....Yes

I then suggested we take a break and the box said 'play music'.

Hannah picked up on a gentleman called Robert who has his own seat up in the gods.

Debra picked up lots of children who also like to be up in the gods.

I decided to take a group onto the 2nd floor and play some music.   I was asking if my gran was with us and had some amazing hits on the k2 meter which spirit can use for yes/no answers.   This goes from green (the weakest) to red (the strongest) and it was flashing up to red every time I asked.   Deep down I knew that my gran would be there, after all she had picked the venue!

I picked up on a man who had a black beard, and I could also smell stale beer.

Janette became aware of a gentleman called Tom Ramshaw and he had a connection with Lily who was maybe his wife.   He was a drunk.

Debra and a group stayed downstairs.

Janette picked up on the ticket person and got the name Maureen and the year 1910.

She also felt that someone had been killed in the hall, maybe by being pushed over the balcony possible by her husband.

The grey lady was sensed, and the group felt that she floats, doesn't walk.   She was an actress, very graceful and the name Ela was given.   Was this Eleanor that was picked up earlier?

They sensed that someone playing a piano, and had a cigarette holder.

Two mediums felt that a young man had had an accident. Debra also picked up on

a man who had to be resuscitated due to a heart attack.

All in all, a fantastic night, lots of evidence given as we were only there a few hours.

The evidence caught on camera was amazing, we had tap responses to questions, most people had their own personal experiences whether it was being touched or smelling something in the room.   Lorraine caught some amazing photos that night including the little boy.   A lady was also caught looking down from the royal box, a family of 3 children were captured on another photo. We also caught what I believe to be Eleanor, as it's a beautiful woman with her hair tied neatly up.

The cctv picked up on some amazing lights, and even picked up on what looks like a bird flying through the wall and disappearing.   All of which can be viewed online.

The local papers printed the story about our investigation and it even made it into the nationals.

The building is absolutely fabulous, steeped in such fantastic history.   Eric (the general manager) also invited us along to investigate the Apollo bingo hall at Durham, which we did and is featured in a later chapter.

A spirit child

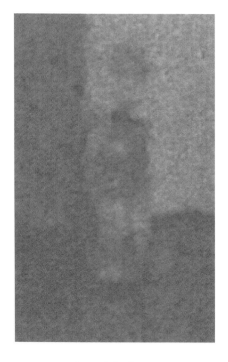

A spirit boy

Is this the Grey lady?

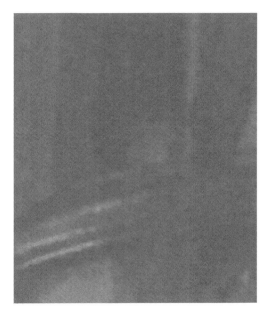

Being watched from the box

Sprit of a lady with baby

SPENNYMOOR BOWLS CLUB

We have previously conducted couple of mini investigations at the bowls club (which was built in 1882 by the co-op) with the spiritual awareness group that used to meet up each week but Rosie (who runs the bowls club) invited us along to do a full investigation as we had caught some amazing evidence.

In April 2017 we set up our night vision cctv equipment and started the investigation.

One of the group immediately became aware of

someone standing on the stairs near the rear doors. This figure was caught on camera and looks like a lady in a black dress with lace sleeves.

Lorraine and Hannah also picked up on a gentleman called Stan, and a man called Frederick who didn't seem to be very nice.

We decided to use the spirit box to see if we could communicate with the spirits in the bar area and things came through straight away. It said 'get out of here' and we picked up what sounded like a very loud breath. It then gave the names Freddy, Peter, Christopher and Phil. It said 'stand up then' at which point all of the group stood up, the it said 'sit' so it looked like they were playing games with us! It even said 'go make a cuppa'.

We were also getting tap responses to questions which also added to the excitement and the name Sally Ann was picked up.

We then moved from the bar area to the bowling area.

Straight away Janette picked up someone who had died in the building of a heart attack, which was confirmed by Rosie.

Everyone had a feeling that they were being watched and people where seeing shadows at the bottom end of the room.

From there we went into the changing rooms where we experienced temperature changes, and lady in her late 30s or early 40s with long brown hair. And a lady with breast cancer was picked up too but this could have been linked with the group.

We then moved onto the lounge, where we were picking up lots of tapping sounds, a man was picked up in the doorway and when I had watched the footage I noticed a shadow that disappeared near to the door. The K2 meter was also lighting up which indicates Electro Magnetic Fields which shows when a spirit is present.

We then decided to take a short break and then split into 2 smaller groups.

After the break I took a group back into the bowling area and Bev and Hannah took a group back into the lounge.

Again, we were picking up shadow figures at the bottom end of the room. As a joke I asked them to make the other group jump, little did I know that this would happen.

We decided to communicate with the talker 2 where it said things like 'near the door', 'something here',' don't go near', 'leave carefully' and 'you are a liar'. We were getting tap and bang responses which seemed to be getting nearer to us.

We then moved down to the bottom area to try our hand at table tipping, and some of the group had great success with this.

In the lounge area the other group were picking up a little boy with a barrow aged between 5 and 7. They got the name Norman, Gerry and Thomas through the spirit box.

One person picked up a lady working in a haberdashery department called Abbie.

Hannah asked Rosie if things like keys go missing as she felt that the spirits of children did this and at this point the burglar alarm sounded as if it had armed itself. This is done via a fob and Rosie was the only one with it. I take this to be because I asked them to make the other group jump, which they certainly did!

It wasn't long afterwards that we decided we should probably call it a night and pack up our things. We were scared incase the burglar alarm was set off again.

The lady caught on the stairs

THE VICTORIA TUNNELS

In November 2016 I decided to book an investigation at the tunnels for 2017.

I'd seen other groups booking it and although I don't usually investigate venues done by other groups, I really felt that we had to do this one. I really didn't know how I was going to cope down inside them as I didn't know if I suffered from claustrophobia! I always check venues out beforehand, but I booked this venue completely blind. But with it being steeped in such history and reputedly haunted we really had to find out for ourselves. It was also something completely different to the buildings we usually have access to.

The Victoria Tunnel is a preserved 19th century waggonway under the city from the Town Moor to the Tyne, built to transport coal from Spital Tongues (Leazes Main) Colliery to the river and operated between 1842 and the 1860s. The Tunnel was converted in 1939 into an air raid shelter to protect thousands of Newcastle citizens during World War 2.

I absolutely love anything linked with the mining community (my grandfather worked down the pit) and anything war related. The spirits are usually lovely and love to communicate with us.

So on Sat 25th March 2017 we all met at the Ouseburn Trust Office, where we were given a health and safety briefing and left our flasks and bags. From there we had a 5 to 10 minute walk to the tunnel entrance, we were given hard hats and torches and sent on our way.

It was incredibly creepy!   The further you went in, the darker and creepier it got.   We were recording with the night vision handycams and immediately started to pick up on the spirits of the tunnel.

A few of the group started to experience chest pain. We sensed a gentleman following us.

Shayna started to get earache, and one of the group had

their arm grabbed.

So far into the tunnels we decided to stand in a group and do a spirit box session but we didn't get much through it, only what sounded like a whimper.

We picked up on a little boy name Jack. We also picked up on a man called Edward, and he was crushed when he was digging the tunnels.

We went further into the tunnel, and still it got darker and creepier. You couldn't help but feel that you were being watched, you also knew that there was only one way in and one way out and it was miles away!

We decided to have a talker 2 session to see if we could get communication going with that.

There was a murmour and it sounded like a man. It said 'who are you', 'airman', 'Mary', 'bowman', 'no you'r not', 'I got laid off', 'be careful'.

Some people in the group started to feel sick and we started to catch orbs on the handycam.

A lot of the group started to smell tobacco, there was definately no one smoking in the group, and we were too far away to be picking it up from outside. We also picked up on a man with a moustache and felt like he was a miner.   A few of us felt very off balance.

We heard a big bang and it sounded like a door closing and we started to hear murmour's and talking in the distance.

We decided to have a break as it had been a very intense session.   Communicating with spirit and walking miles until we got to the end. And you couldn't really see and hand in front of you!

After break some of the group decided to leave as they didn't want to enter again.

So that left us as a smaller group heading back into the tunnel.   Immediately we sensed that we were being watched and we could see a mist in the light of the torch further down the tunnel.

It felt like it was beckoning us deeper into the tunnel. Every time we moved further in, so did the mist.

We went to about the half way point, and started to get tap and noise responses. The talker 2 kept talking about airmen and mentioned the IRA quite a few times, which didn't really make much sense. It also said 'lock the gate',   'we are aware' and 'no way out', which isn't really something you want to hear when your underground.

We decided to try the spirit box again and we got the name 'Fred' and 'Priest'. Some of the group felt like they were drunk on whiskey and I asked spirit if he was a whiskey drinker to which he answered 'no you are'.   It also told us to leave.   We turned off the spirit box and carried on further into the tunnel.

Behind us we could clearly hear footsteps and a male voice echoed.

On our way back to the entrance, Lorraine and I hung back a bit from the group as we kept hearing sounds behind us.   We even heard what sounded like chains being dragged along the floor.   That made us pick up our pace a bit!

Finally we met the rest of the group, and as a parting gift Hannah had a stone thrown at her, which we all heard and we caught on handycam.

I don't believe the spirits of the tunnel meant us any harm, I just think that when a building gets investigated a lot they just get sick.   I know that I would.   They still gave us lots of evidence, I can't imagine what we might have picked up if we had recorded the investigation on cctv but there's no power down there at all.

We took some great photos though, catching what looked like a German Shephard dog, a man wearing a hat and glasses and an amazing photo of a mans face.

It was a fascinating night.   We will definately return with the portal and the full spectrum camera as I'm sure there's still so much to learn about the tunnel.

A man caught in the tunnel

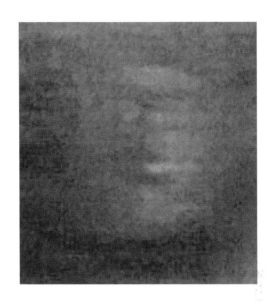

The photo cropped

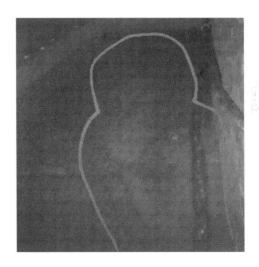

A German shephard dog

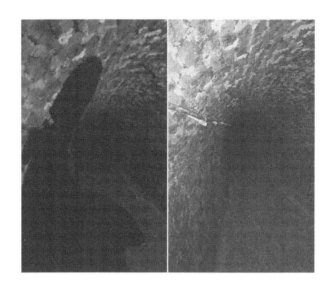

A Shadow figure

Man with glass and a moustache

success.

They moved onto the train carriages and where immediately aware of a conductor with a dog, who was now onboard the train.

There are various taps on the carriages. Hannah picks up on a little girl with a wool coat and plaits. Lorraine picks up her age is 8.

We made our way back to the train carriages where we met up with the other group. They were aware of a lady called Polly and she was there on our last visit earlier in the year and quite a few of the group actually heard her say yes with their own ears.

As Hannah was telling us about Jack and his dog, that looks like a Labrador I started to feel cold around my legs.

The group splits again, my group stay on the train carriage and the other group go onto the bubble cart. The atmosphere had completely changed from the first time they had been on but they still had the feeling that the train is moving.

After a very eventful night we decided to finish the investigation and pack up our equipment.   We caught some amazing photos that night, including the man and boy in the carriage in the car park. Everyone had their own personal experiences, and the people who had never been to an investigation before went away with a better understanding of how spirit work.

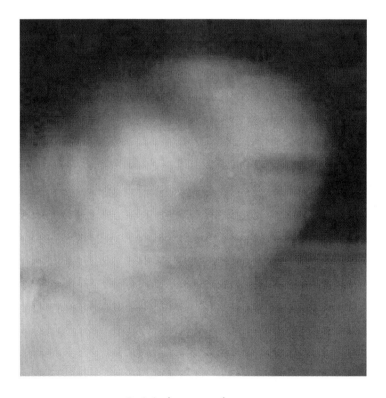

Spirit boy and man

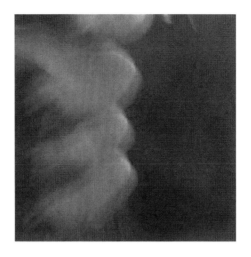

Spooky fingers

Hannah's photo from the 1st investigation

My photo of the Grey Lady?

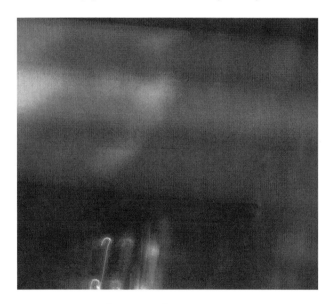

A face in the carriage

fact my eyes should have become more adjusted to it.

We also did quite a bit of spirit photography throughout the evening and Janette caught a fantastic photo of a gentleman underneath the stage.   He was a portly man, wearing a Blue jumper with a cream cap.   He also had a Grey moustache.

Again, Trimdon village hall didn't dissappoint.   A gem of a building, with a fantastic atmosphere.

The man under the stage

Apollo Bingo Durham

The Apollo bingo hall is owned by the Majestic Bingo Limited and we were invited to investigate it following our investigation at the Hippodrome Bingo Hall at Bishop Auckland as it's owned by the same group.　Eric said that the Durham hall is reputed to be haunted and many staff have had their own personal experiences. All of which I kept to myself and didn't disclose to the group.

The bingo hall was originally a cinema and was opened on 29th August 1938.　It was badly damaged by a fire in August 1956 and was closed until December 1956.　The get out, and she spotted a cat walking across the battery.

She went in search of it and it vanished, we later found out that it's actually a spirit cat and not many people get to see it.   Not only did Hannah see it, once I'd watched the cctv footage we had also caught it on film.

Next stop was the watchtower.   The first thing we noticed was that the cctv camera was no longer on the stand but was now on the ground. Once I'd watched the footage back it had been moved several times until it was eventually knocked off.

Inside the watchtower we all felt very uneasy and most of the group felt like they were swaying. Some of the group also started to feel emotional.

Hannah picked up that there is something very important about the morse code machine and a soldier was blown up.   He took a blow to his middle area and then she got the name Miller.

At this point we decided to investigate the cafe. We did a spirit box session, and we found that it really wasn't working too well. But we did keep getting what we could only describe as the sound of a cow bell. We also got some hits on the k2 meter, the energy kept moving around the cafe as we were tracing it as it went.

Next stop was the reception.   We decided to do a spirit box session but again this wasn't working too well so we decided to try the talker 2 device which lets spirit pick random words and make a sentence.   From that we heard 'they are here ' 'come on over' 'where we going?' 'I'll meet you up there' 'you're welcome' and 'do you want to come here'. Some people also felt like they were being touched.

Again, once we had watched the cctv we noticed that the camera had kept being moved again.   Only this time it managed to stay on the stand. We later found out that the spirit in that room doesn't like new things, he even scatters leaflets.

Next we asked Ralph if we could go into the gun room and he gladly took us in there.

We didn't pick up much from spirit in there but Ralph told us lots of info regarding the battery.   We also told him of the various things that we had picked up and he confirmed that they were all correct. He told us about Sgt Miller and his spirit guarding the saracen and that the saracen had in fact been blown up.   The driver was killed instantly and the passenger badly injured to the stomach area. He also told us about the spirit cat.

Finally we went back to the bunkers, this is where we heard the dog barking (there is a german shephard spirit dog), luckily this was caught on handycam and we heard a man whistling a response when we did some calling out.

We also spotted a bell hanging which the soldiers rang if they smelled gas.....this sounded strangely like a cowbell!!!

So, finally after 6 hours of investigating it was time to pack up.   The weather had been extremely kind to us as the battery is very open and on the cliff tops overlooking the sea.

And the spirits had been kind also. Was Heugh battery worth the wait?? Absolutely!

The photo of the adult carrying a child

shooting up.

I had taken some photos on the full spectrum camera and had caught a black child height figure stood next to my keyboard in the hall.   I knew it was a child as it was only as tall as the windowsill.

We decided to move into the middle room.

Dean picked up on a lady who had problems with her breast and felt that this was cancer. She was a slim build and was in her 60s. He described her as a bonny looking lady.

We started another portal session.

It said 'hello' straight away, then laughed.   It said various words including 'wait', 'who's that', and there seemed two voices and sounded foreign, we couldnt make out what it said.

We got the feeling that we were waiting to go into the headmaster's office for the cane.

Some of us felt nervous and some of us felt sick, which is probably how the children felt whilst they sat in the room.

It also said 'who', 'that', 'wow', 'help', 'I know', and 'hey people'.

Dean asked if there's a Pam or Pamela present and the portal responded.

Then a gentleman came through and kept mentioning 'football', we assumed it was sports teacher. We got the name 'Peter', 'don't', and 'that's it'.

We were talking about the difference between teaching today and back in the day and I bet teachers now get more money....the portal said 'I bet'.

I tried to take some photos pointing into the headmaster's office but my camera just kept taking blank photos, but on inspection the morning after there is a face in the darkness and it looks to be a man.

We decided to split up at this point, Dean and Nigel went off into the kitchen and we went into the headmaster's office.

We decided to do some calling out and do spirit photography in this room.   The photos we got were amazing.   We caught a female figure behind on top of the table.   She looked like she had a middle parting but we couldn't decide if it was a young girl or a teacher.

We also caught what looked to be children in the

doorway from the other room.   We also caught a side view of a man with a big nose and large lips stood right next to me in the office.

Dean and Nigel were in the kitchen and were picking up that the temperature had dropped dramatically.   They had a handycam with them and had caught on orb that looked like it was building to something bigger.

Dean feels like there is a man in the room and is feeling quite a lot of pressure to the centre of his head.

Nigel started to feel goose bumps and Dean mentions that the man is stood right next to him. They started to try to get the man to respond and asked who he is. Dean got the date 1846 and they wondered if this was when building was built.   Dean was having difficulty picking things up clearly and things were being blocked. This immediately clearer once he left the kitchen.

At this point we decided to take a break.......after all shayna had brought cake!

After break the ladies decided to venture outside onto the playground and the men stayed where it was warm.

Outside Hannah sensed a lady in the corner near the out building and she was ringing a bell like they would have used back in the day.

On a previous investigation we had caught a little girls face looking down at us from the window, we didn't catch that on camera this time but we did catch a figure stood amongst us.   It looked like an adult but you couldn't make out the gender, just a dark figure.

We ventured back inside to find the men had gone back into the kitchen.

They were trying to talk to the cook and say how easy things are now compared to then.   At that point a huge orb danced across the handycam screen and Dean watched it.

They came out and went into the hall at which point myself, Hannah and Carol went in.

Carol started to feel like she felt a draft, we checked to see if it was coming from the door but it wasn't.   I started to get earache and Hannah felt pressure at the front of her head.

Hannah picked up on the nanny stood at the other end of the kitchen and described her. She said she looks like Mr's Bridges off upstairs, downstairs, has thick beige tights on, all leather shoes with a small heel.   She's wearing a Black dress, charlston length and is wearing a pinny with a pattern on.   She felt the year to be 1920's.

Time has sadly ran away from us so we decided to call it a night.

This night was completely different to the last investigation, there wasn't any darkness this time. Maybe this was due to the fact that there were men in the group this time.

The light anomalies caught on cctv were amazing, and one of the cameras had been turned off and on again twice.   This has never happened before and it was the camera in the headmaster's office.

A young lady caught at Croxdale

A mysterious pair of legs on the playground

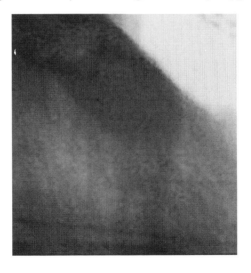

A man wearing a hat

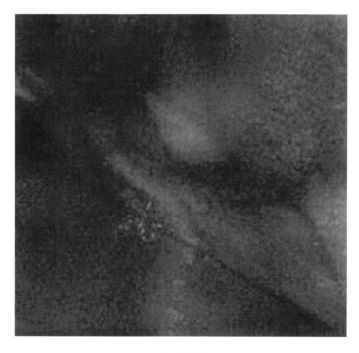

A child

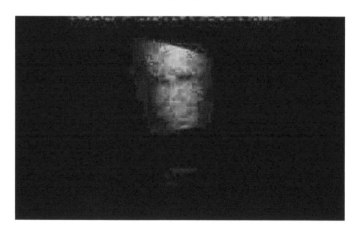

What the camera caught when we thought it wouldn't work!

A figure, stood to the left in the main hall

A gentleman caught on cctv

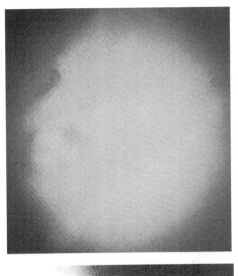

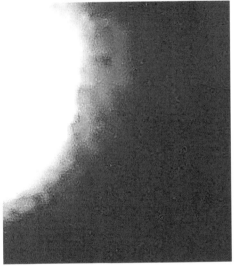

Faces caught on cctv

An orb caught on cctv

A Face caught in the window from a previous investigation

A village Hall in County Durham

I have decided to keep the name of this building anonymous, as I don't want people to stop using it out of fear. It's a lovely building, and would hate the thought of that happening. But I feel like I should share what happened to us there, because of the stupidity of using a oujia board!

Previously on an investigation we all got a little bit freaked out and finished early.

We had all sensed something that wasn't very nice, and we had smelled sulpher which isn't a good sign.   We had also seen the reflection of a man whilst myself and Bev were checking the building was secure before we left.

We were, however, looking forward to returning to see if we could pick up what was lurking in the building.

So in July 2018 we returned, the group was slightly different, Janette wouldn't return and Dean and Lesley joined us this time.

We started in the main hall. People started picking up things immediately.   Some had a bad stomach and headaches, I had a bad ankle and the pain was travelling up my leg.

Dean picked up on two ladies on the stage and a man. The man had difficulty breathing and had something wrong with his throat (possibly cancer). He was slim and is linked to the building. He had a moustache and wore a hat. He had his hands on Dean's shoulders and dean started to feel emotional.

Hannah and Lorraine were watching the stage as it seemed to be getting Darker and they were seeing shadows move across the stage numerous times. It seemed to be getting darker and darker and becoming more active. I also saw something move across the stage too.

I went into the other room to get the portal and as I was coming back into the hall someone stepped out in front of me, I actually thought it was one of the group and jumped out of the way, only the group hadn't moved.

We started working with the portal and after battling to get it to work for a while it started communicating with us. It was saying 'Alf', 'wonderful', 'there he is', 'Jasmine', 'hello', 'behind you', 'Hannah', 'Demon', 'Hey now', and it laughed. It also said 'told you', 'I cant', 'I'm sorry', and 'Sherry'.

I started to sense spirit building up behind Lorraine and Hannah so decided to take some photos with the full spectrum camera (which is a camera which is adapted to capture spirits). The photos that I took revealed lots of spirits behind them, some of them looked extremely creepy!

Hannah started to sense that something not very nice was around and that something was going to happen! She even sat with her hood up.

The portal started to play up again, so Dean changed the batteries and messed around with the settings.

Finally it started to work again.   It said 'please stop', 'no', it also swore at us.   It said 'hello', 'hi', and 'shut up'.   I asked Lorraine if her spirit guide was with her as I had sensed mine was around, which is a comforting thought but slightly worrying.   Lorraine has also sensed her guide's presence too.

We started picking up voices again through the portal, it sounded like 2 men having an argument. It was swearing lots and we did pick up these words...'Bishop', 'she's daft', 'jump' and 'out'.   We also heard screaming through the portal.

Shayna picked up on a man that used to beat up his wife, and Lorraine sensed someone on the ground and someone stamping on his throat.

The portal was now saying 'Im going to kill you', we heard a lady in the background, 'Hannah', a child laughed, 'leave', 'jump', 'jack', 'now', leave', 'get out', 'spectre', 'wipe your boots', 'Derrick', 'come and talk to you', 'feeling sick', 'leave', 'get out', 'devil', 'kill', 'hell', 'intuition', 'sick', 'out now', and 'get out now' in a very angry voice.

We decided to try table tipping which we have never really had much luck with. We do however feel that the table is moving slightly. It seemed to be shaking slightly but not very much else happened.

We all see what looks like a figure standing in the doorway and Dean gets a pain in his neck and down his side but it doesn't feel like a stroke condition.

I went into the back room to get the talker 2. Whilst I was in there I heard something drop, it was very loud but I couldn't see anything.

The talker 2 picked up the words 'Mary', 'I'm not telling you', 'you are a liar', 'no no never', 'who are you', 'what you doing who are you', 'Elaine', and 'be aware'. Was someone trying to warn me about something?   On the stage I felt like singing and entertaining and actually burst out with Hey big spender!

Lorraine felt like she wanted to do the Can Can.   I started getting a pain in the stomach again and Lorraine heard a rustling sound coming from the corridor and came running back on stage.

Nigel heard a breath from the corridor and Bev felt like the top of her head was being touched. A few of us went into the corridor and there was a definate uneasy feeling in there. Like something was lurking in the shadows and was going to pounce at any time.   Our nerves were starting to get slightly shot so we decided to take a break.

After the break, we split into two groups. Dean, Lesley and Hannah went into the back room.   They didnt pick much up in the back room, although there were some light anomalies caught on cctv whilst they were in and they had noticed there was a big drop in temperature.

Meanwhile, the rest of us decided to do another portal session in the main hall.

I asked the portal if someone had done a oujia board within the building and it confirmed that they had.   It also confirmed that it had let an entity in and hadn't closed it properly and it laughed at me.

At this point I said that I didn't think it was funny and that it should go back to where it came from.

Dean, Lesley and Hannah had decided to join us as they heard the portal.

The portal said something that sounded like latin, and said 'pray'. Things then started to take a darker turn and said 'shot', 'get back', 'kill', 'you come', 'help', and you could hear children in the background.

People had started to notice a change taking over my face.......it looked like whatever was lurking wanted to show itself to the group and had chosen me.

There was an evil laugh through the portal, a scream, a child whimpering and an evil laugh.

The whole group had seen the entity change my face. It had pointed ears and a hooked nose and was grinning at them.   I didn't feel anything bad as such but it drained me of energy.   We decided then to close the investigation, say the prayer and finish it with the lord's prayer.

The cctv footage had caught lots of light anomalies in

the building, some of them surrounded us when we were communicating with the portal and one goes into me when the other group saw my features change. We also picked up lots of lights on the camcorder that was set up in the backroom.

A streak of light seems to follow me around, as I'm looking for equipment. It also picked up someone rustling one of the bags.

I think that our guides where around that night as they knew we were going to meet something very strong and negative. They must have felt that as a group we needed to see it, and it just proves my theory about oujia boards. Do not mess with something that you don't know much about and treat it like a toy as it isn't fair on the people responsible for the building.

Something very eerie caught on full spectrum

Floating lady

GHOST WALK AT HAMSTERLEY FOREST

In July 2017 we decided to have our 2nd ghost walk at the wonderful Hamsterley Forest.   We had had some great results the year before, including coming across the phantom horse rider so a few of us decided to take a walk among the trees.

We didn't take the portal that night as its quite heavy, but we did take the spirit box, k2 meters, full spectrum camera and filmed the whole evening via night vision handycam.

After we had walked for a while, we sat on a log amongst the trees and did a spirit box session.

The box was giving us various names, and other words including 'sick' and 'accident'.

Janette picked up on a lady around 65 years of age, she wasn't sure if she was linked to one of the group or the forest.   She got the feeling that she maybe lived in a house in the woods. Janette also connected to a man named Philip.

Hannah saw a lady who was watching us, she was wearing a long Black dress, possibly Victorian in era.

She was about 25 years of age, and her name is Rose. She was collecting sticks for the fire.

We moved on for a little while to another part of the woods. The first thing we noticed was a beautiful robin in the trees. Which I know will be quite common, we were in the woods after all, but they are believed to be messages from spirit!

We started to pick up on spirit again. Hannah felt that the lady in black had followed us and went off to see if she could connect with her.

I sensed that someone had had an accident, a blow to the head and I felt that maybe he was drunk as I could smell stale beer. Nigel also could smell beer.

Hannah felt that maybe someone had committed suicide by hanging in the woods but couldn't get a name. Janette picked up a little boy on a bike who had had an accident. She felt that he went over the handlebars after his bike wheel hit the debris on the floor.

Janette had caught what we all believed to be a man hanging in the trees, but the day after it had mysteriously vanished. I strongly believe that the spirit world wanted us to see it, but not to let anyone else see it. It is someone's loved one after all and the photo was fairly distressing!

We decided to carry on walking, carrying the handycam as we went.   We came along some stone seats.

We sat for a while on the stone seats and I felt great sadness. Hannah felt that the lady was still watching us and there was a little boy called Robin who was connected to her.   Hannah felt that she had another two children, a boy and a girl.

And when Hannah checked the footage, it looks like we have caught a Black figure lurking in the background. Could this be the lady who had followed us all night?

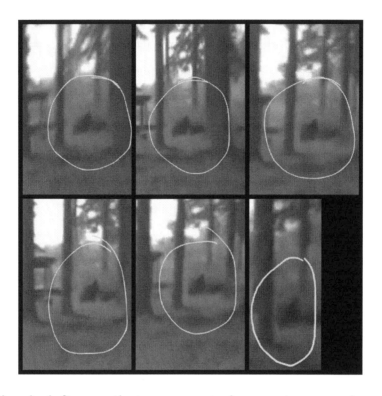

The dark figure, that appears to be moving, caught on handycam

VANE TEMPEST HALL GILESGATE

We have investigated Vane Tempest Hall quite a few times in the past, we have caught various evp's of a gentleman and have had many tap responses.   Evp's are electronic voice phenomemon (voices usually) that are caught on electronic devices like voice recorders. We felt it was time to return to the barracks with the portal and the full spectrum camera in the hope of capturing some amazing evidence and it certainly didn't disappoint.

Vane Tempest Hall was originally called Gilesgate Barracks.   Built in 1863, it served its time as a militia barracks but it was also a smallpox isolation hospital and a mortuary.   There is a courtyard outside that is reputedly haunted, and at the other side of the building there is a cemetery that has its own Grey lady.

Its now used as a community centre, and the outer building are used by different businesses.   For the first time ever we were given access to one of the rooms, that was originally the powder room.

We started the evening as usual, by setting up the night vision cctv cameras. One in the main hall, one in the morgue, one in the passage that joins both rooms and the other right across the courtyard inside the powder room.

We started the investigation in the main room and immediately the cameras started to go in the handycams and the k2 meters. This usually means that it's going to be an active night as spirit build up their energy by draining the batteries.

So, after putting new batteries in everything we started the investigation.

A few of us started to feel sick, and Dawn picked up on a gentleman.   Janette picked up the name Billy who wasn't very happy with us being there.   She was also picking up children in a hospital.

I asked if Billy was the same man that Dawn was picking up on but it wasn't. Janette was picking up on hospital conditions and that amputations would be carried out there.

I did a bit of calling out and immediately began to get tap responses. It actually sounded like one of our metal cases had been opened and closed.

Hannah picked up on a Drill Seargant and he didn't like us being there.

We decided now would be a good time to do a portal session.

The portal session was giving various names including Loui, Jodi, Peter - nothing really of any significance but it did tell us to get out a few times so we turned the portal off.

People were starting to have personal experiences. Jayne saw a dark shadow in the corridor. People were starting to feel cold spots.

We tried our hand at table tipping but nothing

happened. I asked spirit to use all of our energy to make things move or to make a noise.

Janette picked up on the drill sergeant that Hannah had picked up on and said he wouldn't play our games as he's a high ranking officer. He won't take orders off a woman. Guess that's why nothing seemed to be happening with the table and the portal told us to get out.

Nigel tried to get him to give us a response by telling him that he was in the military too.

I picked up that someone had once had a bad ankle as mine started to hurt. We all started to feel really cold, the kind that freezes you to the bone.

I called out to spirit and told them that we are only trying to prove to the world that spirit exist. Janette told us that the sergeant is telling us to get out!

Hannah felt that her throat was tender to the left hand side and extremely dry. Dawn picked up on another energy that strangled a woman. There was a very cold spot in between Hannah and Dawn.

I decided to take some photos on the full spectrum camera and asked if spirit would show themselves.

Janette was starting to feel uneasy and her head was banging.   When I looked at the photos I'd taken there seemed to be a bright light over Janette's face.   She was also starting to become really angry and was swearing a lot which isn't like Janette at all.

Janette moved away and it seemed to move onto Shayna and was changing her features on the photos too.   But luckily it wasn't making Shayna angry.   It looked like it was using the group to show itself, maybe overpowering them somehow.

Hannah picked up that the drill sergeants name was Pip. Shayna picked up the name John James, and Dawn had gotten the name James earlier on in the evening.

We decided to use the talker2, which is like an ovilus. It gives out random words, and it sounds like a robot. The only problem with a talker2 is that it speaks very quiet so you can't really make out what it says until you watch the footage later on.

Once we'd watched the footage it showed that the talker2 was talking about airmen, and was answering our questions. It was talking ejecting from a plane, and was talking about Red house. And it said 'they are in the air'. Some of the group picked up on the name Kenneth.

I decided to look up Red House, and there was an auxiliary hospital for ww1 soldiers somewhere near to London. Could he have been talking about that?

I decided to do some spirit photography and we caught some amazing photos. It looked like something was in front of Janette's face shrouding it. Could this have been the spirit that was making her angry. Shayna's face also had changed, she had taken on male features and looked like she had a bald head. Her head also looked out of proportion with the rest of her body.

I also got a photo of a man's face, side on, and it was an amazing photo.

We decided to move into the other hall (which apparently used to be a small pox isolation hospital and a morgue. Just as we were moving Hannah heard a loud groaning in her ear and earlier on that evening I had heard a grown in front of me in the corridor.

As we were in the corridor Dawn felt a cold spot. She also picked up on a chaplin in the hall. When Janette entered the room she saw a child in the corner of the room. And she was feeling very emotional.

The room was absolutely freezing. It's a big room with a polished wooden floor and a big old doorway which apparently they used to take the bodies out of.

Janette also mentioned feeling jaw ache which both myself and Bev had also experienced. And she was picking up children again and was feeling emotional.

Hannah told us that she was aware of a soldier looking out of the upper window toward the graveyard. It used to be two storey as you can see the upstairs windows and doorway so maybe the hospital was on the top floor and morgue on the bottom. I would love to see an old photo of it, maybe Jessica (the caretaker) will find out more info as she's looking into the history to put onto the website.

We decided to have a portal session. It gave the name 'peter' and 'Geoff'. I said I would like to speak to Pip and its replied 'can't be done'. Shayna asked 'Did you get smallpox?' it replied 'no'. Janette asked 'don't you want us here?' it replied 'go'. She also asked 'how long were you here for?' it answered '5 years'. She asked 'are there children here? It answered 'don't tell her!' 'are there many of you here? It answered 'probably 71'.

I did some spirit photography in this room and was picking up mysterious bright streaks of light on most of the photo.

We decided to have a break, we needed to warm ourselves up!

After the break we decided to tackle the powder room and grounds but we split into two groups as the room isn't very big.

My group went in the room and the others went to the graveyard and grounds. Nigel got a headache as we went in.

We did a portal session and straight away it shouted 'Get out!' and was swearing at us. Infact for most of the session it was shouting the same things over and over. He really didn't want us in the room. It also kept stopping the spirit box. We did keep hearing a lady in the background but the angry man wouldn't let her speak to us.

Nigel asked if they were in the queens navy, at which he didn't get a response, so he then asked if they were in the infantry and it replied 'yes'.

I tried to take some spirit photography but I just kept getting a blank screen, he really didn't want to show himself to us in any way.

The other group were outside and as we were swapping

rooms Nigel said 'here's another group for you to shout at' and it responded 'true'.

Hannah told us that they had as they were walking in the grounds near the graveyard they kept seeing a mist which suddenly appeared from nowhere.   Jayne managed to catch it on camera. Shayna felt a bit unerved.   My group didn't feel anything outside and unfortunately didn't see the mist.

They headed back to the courtyard and had a walk around the upper rooms outside.   They picked up on a soldier who was a big guy.   He used to watch the buildings. They touched the doors and could feel the different energies coming from the rooms.   One of them didn't feel very nice.

They carried on with the portal session and were getting various responses including 'I'm starving' and 'bread'.

Jayne didn't like it in the room, and it was extremely dark.

Hannah sensed the man in the room and Dawn felt like someone was behind her. They picked up that the man was very angry but was also sad.   Dawn felt as though he wasn't wanted by his family and Hannah felt like he had Post traumatic stress disorder and that he was very nervous. She felt like the room was oppressive and could feel pressure on her head.

As they were trying to leave they couldn't get the door open.   It seemed like someone was pulling it from the other side.

We headed back into the main building and a couple of us decided to do a little vigil upstairs in the tower. Hannah sensed a soldier stood behind me who was really tall.   He was linked to the tower and Hannah told me to take some photos behind me.   Again, on the photos were very bright streaks of light.

We went back into the first hall as time was passing by very quickly.   As we were sitting we heard cries through the baby monitor.   Hannah and I went in to investigate whilst the other sat and listened.

We heard a noise coming from the back corner and whilst we were in the room the others could hear two men talking and a baby screaming.   We return to the group and I turn the volume up on the monitor and it sounded like men screaming out in agony.
Unfortunately this was too quiet to be caught on handycam but next time we investigate there I will keep a voice recorder close to it in the hope of picking up the

sounds.

I know that baby monitors can pick up sounds from other monitors and this could explain the baby crying but it why would it pick up the sounds of men screaming and talking?

It was very unerving. But it was a fabulous investigation.

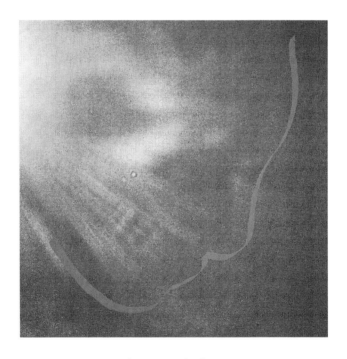

The man's face

In the mortuary

TRIMDON GRANGE COMMUNITY CENTRE

Trimdon grange community centre is situated in the heart of an ex-mining village.

The building is over 100 years old and was once infact a school, here all local children attended.   The community centre is not only used for activities, it is also home to the minders banner from Trimdon Grange Colliery – a great piece of history.   And it has pride of place in the IT Suite.

We are extremely lucky to have investigated the community centre quite a number of times now.   Each investigation has been fantastic, it has a lovely feel to it and the evp's that we have caught are some of the best in our history of investigating.

On 7th October 2017 we returned to investigate, the current group have never investigated it before and we had a full house!

Shayna picked up on a boy called Timmy with Blonde hair and Blue eyes, and she picked up that he might have suffered from epilepsy.

We were hearing a strange noise in the room, I thought it was down to the large clock in the room but when I went to check it out it wasn't.   I couldn't find out what the noise was but it sounded strangely like someone was using breathing apparatus.

We did a portal session and straight away it was giving the names 'Bill', 'Mark' and 'Russell'.   We asked if there were any teachers in the room and were given the name 'Mr Robson'.

We were given the names 'Luke'and 'Billy'.   Jo's chair was pushed from behind, which made her jump!

Dean sensed a man watching us and another man and he felt that his chest was crushed.   He felt that he was a grandfather and asked if he was linked to one of the group.

Hannah and Lorraine were freezing cold and sensed there were two children stood at the back of the room.

We heard a noise outside of the room like kids running in the corridor, and both Hannah and Lorraine went to investigate it only Lorraine couldnt open the door.

We were still hearing the strange breathing sound, and it sounded like an iron lung from days gone by.

Janette was picking up the name Billy and someone was saying 'our Billy'.

I decided that I would get the spirit dice out. We laugh about it being called spirit boggle but we have had some great success with this in the past. And spirit children seen to like it as they think it's a game. Spirit dice have letters on them, we shake them in a bag and tip them onto a surface. Spirit can use them to write their name or random words. You are supposed to go with the first word or name that you see. But the problem is, if you have a large group you tend to all see something different.

We were getting the names – Lil, Dan, Betty, Susan, Doris, Gavin and Lou.

We decided to put the portal back on whilst using the dice in the hope that we could match the two.

We were recording it all on handycam and we captured an orb going over the portal. It said the name 'Bobby', said hello, and 'Bobby is a bugger'. It also said 'be attacked' in an incredibly creepy voice.

It said 'sick', 'Im gone,' We here', 'its not me', and 'Lisa'. Then something was thrown in the room, it sounded like a stone and it landed on the wooden floor.

It gave out a few more names and gave a funny laugh. It looked like the kids were having fun with us. There was also a funny kind of breath caught on handycam like something was very close to us.

After a short coffee break we decided to split into two groups. Bev took Dean, Lesley, Carol, Nigel, Shayna, Lou and Mark into the Banner room and I took the rest back into the main hall to have a go at table tipping.

Shayna was linking with a man who she felt had died of a heart attack. Dean picked up on a couple. She was head teacher and they were husband and wife. The man had suffered with high blood pressure.

Carol was feeling very cold all down her right side and Dean decided to do some calling out.

Bev went into the 2nd main room with Lou and Mark.

Dean and the others joined them not long after.

They did a portal session and again were picking up the names 'Tom', 'Spence', 'Steven', 'doctor', 'I'm back', and various other words.   It also laughed.

Dean started to feel a bit sick and he heard a bell ring. He also picked up on a lady who passed away from falling down the stairs at home.

We did some table tipping in the main hall and very little happened but we did still hear the breathing noise but still couldn't work out where it was coming from.

We moved into the banner room as the other group had finished in there and Lorraine felt that crossed words have been said in that room.   Hannah and I picked up on a dog in the room and we both felt that it was a labrador.

Hannah told the group that as we were setting up earlier she picked up a man with a bad chest and he was a miner.   He was approx 49 years old, with a moustache, his skin was well weathered and he was wearing a tweed jacked and knitted waistcoat.

Janette picked up the name Charlie, but liked to be called Charles.

Lorraine said that she felt that the crossed words were over some money that had gone missing either from a charity box or a locked box.

Hannah felt that the building had been on the verge of closing more than once.

Hannah was picking up on a teacher who was an old spinster. She felt that none of the kids liked her. Janette picked up the name Martha and felt that it was the same woman.

Janette said the teacher coudnt stand thick kids, infact her words were she couldnt tolerate thick shits! She felt that she would be cruel to certain children, she used to hit them with her ruler.

Lorraine picked up on a lady who hated to come to work as a man used to be a pervert and he used to rub up against her at any opportunity.

We decided to move into the 2nd main hall but very little happened, we even tried the portal but not a single word was spoken through it. What I didnt realise is the other group thought we had finished and had told spirit it was time to go. Guess they had all cleared off by the time we went into the room.

Again, a fantastic investigation. The spirits of Trimdon Grange were very accommodating and welcoming. But it goes to show that they don't hang around, they just pop back to visit and work with us and then when its time, they go back to the spirit world.

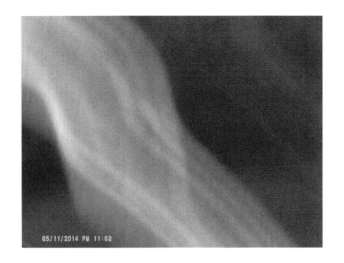

Mysterious lights caught on camera

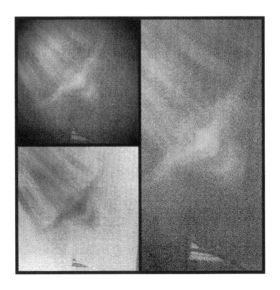

Caught on stage

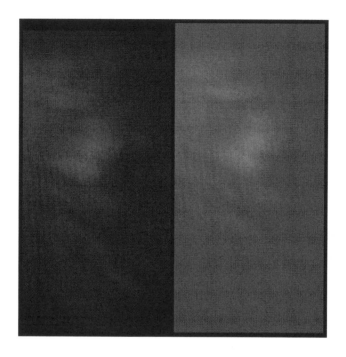

Could this be the labrador?

THE FIFTEAS VINTAGE TEAROOMS

The tearooms are situated in part of the former Mount School, which started teaching in 1864 until it closed in the 1960s. It's a fabulous building steeped in history but also has a tragic past.

But the building has a wonderful atmosphere, and anyone visiting the Bishop Auckland areas should definitely visit for a cuppa and cake.

I approached the tearooms earlier in the year and Becky agreed to let us investigate.   They were keen to find out who they kept seeing in the kitchen.

A figure stood at the back watching them and they kept seeing things out of the corner of their eye.   They weren't bothered by it but wanted to see if we could find out who it was.

We did our investigation on Friday 19th October and were welcomed by Jude, Becky and Neve. They really did go to extreme lengths to make us welcome, even putting black out sheets on the windows to make sure it was dark enough. And the coffee was to die for!

So we set up camera in all areas that we felt were the most active and talked the ladies through what would happen.   I could tell from the start that it was going to be a great night as the ladies where so excited about it and were fazed by it at all.   Spirit can always sense the atmosphere and if there is very little fear within the group always step forward to communicate. Usually if there are new people in the group who have never been on an investigation before they do things more subtly so that they don't scare people off.

So, we started the investigation in the main tea room at the front of the building. You immediately got the feeling that you were being watched and the mediums picked up the name Bobby.   Hannah picked up a figure of authority and she also picks up a soldier and Lorraine got the name Andrew.

I picked up a man with a tiny bit of facial hair just under his chin and a lady that had suffered with breast cancer in her left breast.   Hannah picked up on a man who had sideburns and was maybe a teddy boy.

There started to be the odd tap and bang coming from the room as I was doing some calling out, asking spirit to communicate with us.

Lorraine picked up two little girls who were sisters with Pollyanna hair syles and cut off fringes.

I picked up a dog and felt that someone was stood right in front of me.

We decided now would be a good time to do a portal session and immediately it began to give us names. We picked up 'Philip', 'Melissa', 'speak', and 'listen'.

The name Melissa kept coming through so clearly she was quite willing to talk to us. I sensed that we were being watched from the back of the room, the portal confirmed this when it said 'standing at the back'.

Hannah was picking up a soldier from the 1st world war, or at least that's how he showed himself.

I jokingly asked spirit if they pinched the cakes?   It laughed and said 'from the fridge'.

Lorraine sensed that Melissa had passed with an asthma attack and asked the portal if that was correct. Her answer was 'can't go there'. The gentleman in the portal also said that he's pissed off.

There was a gentleman kept saying 'help us', and a lady said 'goodbye'.   We asked if there was anyone linked to the school and it said 'peoples school'.

Melissa came through the portal again and said that she's in heaven.

We caught quite a few orbs on handycam around the portal and you could tell that the spirit energy was very strong.

The portal started to sound like a few people in the spirit world were having a conversation among themselves but we couldn't make out what they were saying.

Lorraine picked up on a little boy who had drowned in the river.   Hannah picked up on a reverend that had lots to do with the school.   He used to do the RE lessons and she felt that some of the girls from the school would be taken to the castle on a Sunday.

She also picked up that the uniform was a pinafore dress, boots and they looked really posh!

We decided to move to the back room and carry on the investigation there. We immediately started to pick up sadness, Shayna was getting hip pain so asked spirit to take it away.   Sometimes spirit can put a feeling on you (usually something that they suffered with in life, or even how they passed) and if you ask them to step away the feeling goes.

Carol mentions sickness and a pain in the chest and I pick up a spirit in the room who used to suffer with indigestion.

Hannah picked up with a lady who wore her hair in a bun, but couldn't pick up anything else.

Jude and Becky started to tell us about the dance school and the floor above us, as Hannah felt that there was quite a bit of activity up there.   We could all feel the difference in energy from this room to the last one.

The ladies also told us about the shadow of a man that is seen in the kitchen.   Hannah felt that he has a mischievous side but he doesn't mean any harm.   She picked up that he was a world war one soldier, and his uniform is made of scratchy material and he wears leg wraps.

Hannah noticed the dress in the corner of the room and started to talk about a lady that she felt was broken hearted and was supposed to marry the soldier but he didn't make it home.   Jude said that the dress was a replica of ones worn in the 1930 or 40s so it couldn't really have any links to the lady, but maybe the lady wore dresses very similar. Hannah also got the name Amelia. Lorraine felt that the lady didn't get to wear a dress, maybe a wedding dress.

We decided to try the dowsing rods and hold a portal session.   The words that came through the portal were 'resting', 'Dennis', 'Tilly', 'cheat', 'hello', 'Ed', 'Melody', 'la,la,la' and a laugh.   The responses weren't as good as we had gotten in the first room but it had a completely different atmosphere.

We decided it was time to head into the kitchen, where the shadow figure was often seen.

Jude was telling us about when she is making jam she sometimes sees a shadow figure on the stainless steel fridges and has gone to look only to find there's no one there.

We didn't really have much response in there, but there

were quite a few light anomalies caught on cctv.   There were some spikes on the emf detector (K2 meter) too but there's lots of electrical equipment in there which could be the cause.

We decided to take a break, and during the break we somehow got talking about Reiki therapy.   Reiki is a Japanese technique for stress reductiona nd relaxation that also promotes healing. A lot of our group are Reiki attuned and some are Reiki masters.   I myself am Reiki 2 attuned and decided to give the ladies a little taster of what it's like to have a treatment and told them a little bit about peoples aura.

I believe your aura is an important part of investigating as you feel lots through it. And I believe it helps you to understand when a spirit draws close to you.

After the break we split into groups, some of the ladies went into the pink room near to the toilets.

They didn't really get much of a response when they tried a portal session and then they moved into the reception part with the fireplace.

There was a bit more of a response there.   The portal said 'Cane', 'nasty', 'Stuart', 'Audra', 'Cath' and goodnight.

Were they talking about having the cane at school and it being a nasty punishment?   We took it that we were coming to the end of the investigation at that point as they were saying goodnight.

Whilst they were investigating this room, some of the group were watching the cctv monitor and I was carrying out a lone vigil in the back room.   From there I did some spirit photography in the kitchen where I caught these amazing photos.

Becky at this point was starting to fall asleep in the chair, I guess the Reiki treatment had relaxed her a little too much!!

It was a fantastic investigation at the Fifteas vintage tearooms.   An absolute gem of a building, steeped in history with some lovely spirit visitors.

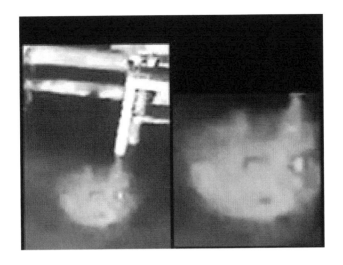

A face caught on cctv in the first room

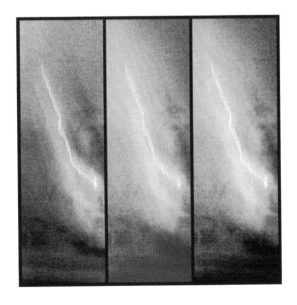

The face caught in the second room

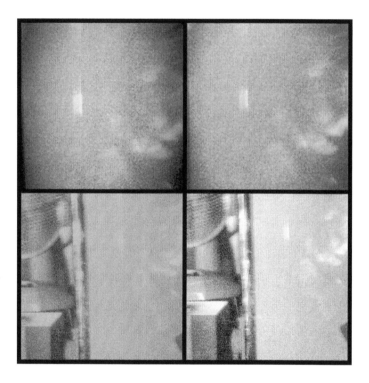

The face of lady sideways in the kitchen

I hope you have enjoyed our account of what happened on our paranormal quest.   The buildings that we have included in this book are really a small fraction of the fabulous venues we have covered of the last six years. Please remember that this is what happened on each visit, whether you believe it's paranormal or not is really up to you, but I believe that the evidence we have caught should at least make you think that maybe there is something out there.

Each venue has had a list of the evidence and footage caught so that if they so wish they can research any information that we have picked up. Unfortunately, I don't have the time to do this for them.

A big thank you to the venues for giving me permission to include them in the book.   We have lots more to look forward to next year, which we will hopefully include in the next book.

All cctv footage from each investigation is available to view via social media, but if you would like to contact me the email address is spectredetectors@yahoo.co.uk where I will happily send you the links.

Printed in Poland
by Amazon Fulfillment
Poland Sp. z o.o., Wrocław